inlays
Stash Luczkiw

CHIT

Copyright © 2015 by Stash Luczkiw
Book design by Diwani E. Fatatis

All rights reserved. Except for brief passages quoted in a newspaper, magazine, radio or television review, no part of this book may be reproduced in any form or by any means, electronic or mechanical, including photocopying and recording, or by any information storage and retrieval system, without permission in writing from the author.

ISBN 978-1507801406

for Caterina

inlays

S̲t̲a̲s̲h̲ L̲u̲c̲z̲k̲i̲w̲

contents

The Passionate Years 1

embedded traces 3

We nomads at times 5
Europa Repose 6
In Extremis 7
celebrate 8
Caterina 9
The Days Between Us 10
If we 11
Where is Love? 12
Alone Now 13
In your portrait 14
Your skin 15
Matrix 16
For My Son About to Be Born 17
Baby don't 18
Ruben 19
Boy on a Bike 20
Two Boys on the Beach 21
Stuff My Kids Fill the House With 22
Up River 23

an emptying 25

blood oranges and artichokes 43

Lago di Como 45
Easter Basilica 46
Mediterraneo 1 47
Mediterraneo 2 50
Quadri Toscani: Monte Cetona 53
Portofino 55
Love in a Tuscan Light: Easter Sunday 61
Blue 64

Rocks 1 70
Rocks 2 71
Rocks 3 72
Rocks 4 73
Ruins at Seliunte 74
Anonymous Painting 75
Each evening's history 76

conditions 79

If I found blood in this rock 81
The Telling 82
Opium 83
Watching the Welder 84
The Old Bricklayer 85
The Jewel 86
Three Ways of Describing a Persimmon 87
You are beautiful but 88
Verse in Search of an Anthology 89
Baudelaire 90
After Creeley 91
After Derrida 92
Nowhere Near Pont Mirabeau 93
After Tolstoy 95
Waterfall 96
The Lure of the Exotic 98
Ten-year-ago Photo 99
Insight 100
Gloria in Paris 101
Conversation with a Writer 102
Waiting for the Yellow Buses 103
Tato 107
Figure at the Top of the Stairs 108
Moving Again 109
I have seen glimpses of an eye 110
Metastasis 111

Airports and the Thing That Smells Like Fear 112
An Afternoon with Andy Warhol
and Abu Musab al-Zarqawi 113
If I Told You Death Was Just 114
Because the sun 115
On Leaving 116

dependent redemptions 119

Who woke up this morning 121
In dream 122
Change Up 123
No 124
Dependent Redemptions 125
Learning language as if 126
The language that sustains 127
After Ibn Arabi 128
After Psalm 104 129
"Which of the Lord's bounties
do you and you deny?" 130
Lord 131
Jesus 132

things here 135

The Passionate Years

These are the passionate years:
of blood oranges and artichokes,
of bed sheets stained with love.

Years of cryptic languages chanted in the dark,
on my knees, in a room full of toys belonging
to boys who dream in tongues.

When I was young there was passion,
but I was still reaching to be free
of what now hails down on me.

There was the struggle between angel
and animal, between askesis and the steed.
Now hunger and urge have won out.

These are the passionate years,
when we are back to believing in God—
lighting candles under a vault of ancient bricks,

kissing the feet of bleeding statues.
In these years of fear for our future we are
again killing innocents in the name of an idol.

In these passionate years of sowing
souls, holding houses and taking hostages,
violence comes of its own accord; and I pillage

and plunder from the mountains to the sea,
and meander through my cities—an assassin
armed only with the thorns of ideas.

Yet I know at some point I must surrender
this tract of flesh to your passion,
Lord… I only ask, *Would it be blasphemy*

to say: "Your suffering is so sweet!"?

embedded traces

———//———

We nomads at times
long for the still life,
immovable and permanent—
as much as is possible
in a turning world.
We long for a table
that knows all
we use to fuel us,
a stable foothold
to keep us on our feet.

But as soon as we
are on our feet it seems
the path beneath us moves;
and though we are at rest,
the landscape rides past us
to inform our wandering minds—
our nature—of the nature
of our solidarity.

We long for a bed,
a bed of earth
in which to rest,
in which to turn
and love each moment's end
as if it were our own.

Europa Repose

Still wings span
the foreign landscape:
seek a soft, sedentary
refuge in history.

Here the hordes
no longer ravage (for
now), heretical heads
no longer roll

in any sense
that is literal.
Here a mechanism
of pleasure upholds.

The first function
of culture is
to bridge with skill
the irreparable rifts.

Sunflowered roads
over mass-grave sites,
crosses where sacred
wells have sprung.

The prey now hides
in posed museums.
One pays and admires—
to beautify the wounds.

In Extremis

To love is the most
extreme act one can undertake
in life. How then is it possible
to love and not be happy?
Is there something in extremes—
like the flirt with death,
a junky whine, or a mercenary
smirk—that belies contentment?
Something that flouts
the possibility of wanting
exactly what you have?
Maybe we all need to simply
trash our sweeping statements
and come to terms with pain—
love or no love, on the edge
or in the same old mire.

celebrate

the skin
that separates
us
grows more
supple
in the song

Caterina

I poured the soup
for two.
          You've only
been away one day.

The Days Between Us

In 5 days
(or in 20 or 12)
we'll be alone
again, and we'll be well.

You'll be swimming
in blue pools,
and I'll be digging in
circles I spun out from
in the beginning.

In 5 days
(or in 50 or 3)
you'll be gone
to take care of your boy,
and I'll be trying
to be a boy no longer
and still be free.

In 5 days
(or in 90 or in 2)
I'll be thinking again:
"What would it be like
to be only with you?"

if we
could only
become
one mind
as we
become
one body
then everything
would be
so much
simpler and less
bearable

Where is Love?

All the books
missing from this shelf
testify
to a flight:

from ideas
to the bitter grind
of physical necessity.

Where is love
left in pages
dog-eared and glossed
with margins
full of cryptic notes?

What is left
of it in sheets
stained
with an absent lover?

Alone Now

The sweat-
drenched bed
smells sweet—
same as when
my liver purged
all the bile
built up
in wandering
into you.
We talked
and fought
last night,
in essence
about not being
able to talk,
about unsaid
essentials
and misreading
intentions
in the light
of a fragile trust.
So we bit
each other
and made love,
saying things
such as can
only be said
amid an odor
of violence;
and I came
in you and
stayed there
and you licked
me clean
of your blood
and we fell
asleep finely.

In your portrait

I watch
the reflection
of roof tiles
that were red
before you left
into the snow…

now white
and thick
in the richness
of your scent.

———//———

Your skin
against mine
dissolves
whatever walls
rise
between us

Matrix

Your scar,
slit width-wise
against my longing
to be alone,
holds a tome
of palpable flesh,
blood and bone.

Your creation, written
on the hearer's soul,
bears me to a new
birth I enter
willing yet wary—
for fear
of not listening,
of only pretending
to hear how
your winged lips
inviting me
through them
into your womb
have the force
of madness which passes
as prophecy—
speaking for
a life you nurture,
a life I am
unable to sustain
with anything but
a passion reflected
on paper
that will outlive me.

For My Son About to Be Born
after Vasyl Stus

Where will I get the faith
to raise you with your brother?
In harmony. I've prayed
in the highest mountains
for my way to clear itself
of me, to be empty. And still
I rage through days I feel
are no longer my own,
tremble in a body hungry
for solitude, held together
by violent hands terrified of holding.
I remember beyond the tree line,
under the peaks, where a solitary
wild flower gazed at me,
surrounded by lichen and stark rock.
I picked it and put it in
my book—the book too full of me,
written simply, off-hand and childless
for the sake of seeking.
How those dense convolutions soothed!
Now time is my nemesis. The time
that was mine must pass away
as the days inform your coming
struggle. This fear is so basic.
Life assails one exactly
where one longs to be free.
For this affront I lack faith.
Because I know somewhere
you will be too full of me:
always longing to be alone
on the way to being all one.

Baby don't

jump
out the window

If
you fall you
won't

be live

enough
to enjoy
the echo of

your scream

Ruben

I was standing outside on the terrace
thinking "what a struggle to transmit
the imaginal world into this physical one
with language" when I saw you walk by.

You were carrying the plastic basketball
I got you in Istanbul, looking for the hoop.
I found it and stuck the suctions to the fridge,
then said, "Hold on, I have to make a note."

A few dunks while I wrote were enough
to make you hungry, and you asked to be fed.
As I guided the spoonfuls into your mouth
I told you about some unseen angels I've met.

Boy on a Bike

My heart quickens
when he goes too fast
or heads for a hole:

eyes like training wheels,
back tire spinning out
dead leaves between them.

Two Boys on the Beach

Careful in those waves,
boys. The ocean is
a sweet beast of relief.

It'll lick you clean
and swallow you
whole. Forever.

And with my eyes
full of wind
and sand, the words

that make me
lose themselves
in the page's glare.

Stuff My Kids Fill the House With

Hollow Easter eggs at the end of a stick in a pot of dirt.
A baked clay pencil holder.
An elephant bookmark.
Biscuits from last year's trip to their grandmother still
 wrapped in plastic.

Gathering dust
on the piano, behind the bed, on every spare bit of shelf
 space:

special non-slip socks—
 one here, one who knows where...

a general mess echoing the silence
when they're not around
and the rainwater in the gutter
and me saying "Shit!"
when I step on a loose piece of Lego.

Up River

The rapids well up into waves,
crash against the scattered rocks
and stray boulders, then ebb away,
quietly containing the flow
of handholding thoughts
that lead to images of loss
on my way down to the banks:
the sand rising up in ribs with the breeze
swooping down from the mountains,
lambent whisks of melancholy,
geese flying by in V-formations,
the sun veiled by desultory clouds,
gnats hovering in a pocket of heat
that forms above an inlet's eddy
while an ass cools off under a tree.

Thoughts of how I might not see you
again have brought me here to relive
the one fearless moment
when I marry you—again. And again
I'd put my finger through your ring
even here at Lethe's banks,
where I'll forget all I've made with you
before in order to be blessed once more
with that first sight—and get it
just a little more right each time.

an emptying

Let go
the handholding need
your full glass
refracts

before umbilical blood
fills
the chalice you will
forget to quest for.

The dread cusps
of some
hypothetical unknown
edge
against the rails:

glint-locked
appendages of comfort
waning with innocence.

Should you see
the peripheral slit
center you
back onto birth-track,

yield only
if the absence
therein be
as it is when
not.

Concrete eats
the forms your face
indulges in
with no mirrors around.

The senseless
morphs
your anemic mother tongue
abstracts in dream will
lick clean
the covet-stones
between your temples.

Change
for change's sake
stills
the desert breast's
plangent anguish.

You climb
this sand scree
when feet are metaphor
and the mine
a field of possible
implosions.

Listen
to your drift-beat's deft
inflection
when the anodized sky's
film
succors
these frenetic twists
of restlessness
into rigid
idiom.

Dig into
genitive divisions
you qualify
in meaning what's
hardly heard.

Cross-rites
counter Adam-wrath's
light-bear
investiture.

Till this earth-
mother of a task
with labor pain and
fists full of lyrics.

Dance as one
essence with light
heaving
through its endless
working out.

Translate all
you hear
into an aftermath,

till the sound
becomes almost
a system,
stiff with rigor.

Then find the
silence…
source of
your comprehensive
exhaustion.

On mild Advent evenings
the streets
that criss-cross
your neighborhood
will leave you

looking in store windows
to buy
what relieves
only in the wanting,

for
in the having it
betrays
the eyes as dead ends.

Bathwater flotsam
reflects
domestic trials.

Lint sifted
from inexhaustible pockets
piles up
to utter a word

where you would leave
or let
it all go
in the turbid work.

Take the foot
that sets
the time in motion
and hold, push
ever
so slightly
on the point

where, in love's
fulfillment,
a quiet moment shared

hones the blunted
virtue
of human touch.

If jaw locks shut
and tongue blocks
fricative lips, and
the one
you call on to be
there plays dumb,
then… what?

Nothing, but dream
an open ear.

Holding the tender
trade offered
as sacrificial
duty.

A commerce of gestures
may have to suffice
where what's on paper
won't wipe
tears of fever
and night fear.

Note well the writing
wedged into moments
between
the time I hold
you and the
names I litter
my journal with.

If I could just shaft
a light through
to your sealed eyes,
open
them and lift
your illness,

would I remain longer?

And if I broke
your face (a condition
of possibility) with
the stuffed rage
that keeps me
stuck
into pieces, what
would love (in its
condition) deem probable?

A face lost
in fragments,
unfit to express
the barest emotion
for its
incongruous tenses,

subjoined in a mood
no longer available,
contingent on
an inept reading of
my blow.

The first slivers of light
loitering under the door
initiate

an emptying
of the overfilled room,
laden with passages
relegated to an oblivion
behind broken lips
hushed with wonder
and pursed
at the prospect
of a new alternative:

bookshelves boxed
and stuck into cracks
the wall has opened
for nothing's sake.

blood oranges and artichokes

Lago di Como

We nomads know
motion. Moving
through mirror lakes
buried deep under
mountains no houses know,
through strange landscapes
we appropriate with our
own absence of familiarity,
ferried across the broken
reflection of time the lines
on our faces convey.
These are the passages
that make us a way
the still-born world holds
at arms length, warring
with the same arms
that hold us in judgement.

We move to know
what we are not,
owing only what
we cannot hold
in a world that won't stop.

Easter Basilica

Skin smells burnt from sun's first rays.

A long winter it was.

Dogs chase each other around ruins—Roman columns.

Ruben raising hell, throwing rocks with a bigger girl, running just to run.

Misha nursing in the shade of an olive tree, suckling at C's breast, under the canopy of her hair.

We wait for mass to end, to see the ashes of a dead friend.

I would have missed all these scenes if I'd continued running without realizing

I was always headed for this...

* * *

In the sacristy:
what's left of a pagan sacrifice chamber:
mosaics and ashes
waiting for their proper place.

Mediterraneo 1

The oleander road
                      leads to a gravel path
that takes us to the shore
                            at cliff's edge
where we watch, facing a head-wind,
      the waves below
                                  crash
into rock faces
                once inspired me to recite
their rhythms
                      filtered through the Poem's light.

I tried at sunset to remember an ocean verse
once held by heart, one of the few
I knew in the language that nursed me, a language
I now reserve for prayers with my boys.

I'd forgotten the last stanza and struggled
with my memory as the wind whipped
my hair back and in my arms the boys
squinted, trying to hear the sun touch the water.

How many lines have I lost
        in the time taken to raise
                      real blood and bone children?

The images I sacrifice around me: a sapphire sea,
wave crests roiling against a salt-worn shore,
agaves that blossom once every several
generations
above the rugged scarp...
                            Specific scents:
erisimo. How long have I searched for this word
only to be told of names in a number of dialects
when I needed it in my own rootless English,
or at least in the great Tuscan's tongue (though
I doubt the singers' herb grows in Tuscany,

and may well be indigenous
only to *the meadow made-up by the mind,*
that is not mine, but is a made place,
that is mine, it is so near to the heart...)?

Barren hillocks watched by abandoned towers
used by Christians to safeguard the coast against
Saracens. Mushroom-shaped cement bunkers
left by Nazis...
                and sea urchins...
                                and starfish...

All this and more
        fodder
                for parts of poems that
won't fit
between the prose and daily chores.

While cooking lunch, between
        cutting tomatoes
                and pitting olives,
I read aloud,
    in the light of my lady's caramel skin,
        an extract from Williams' *Asphodel.*
Toward the end
        where he says:
                Don't think
that because I say this
    in a poem
        it can be treated lightly
or that the facts will not uphold it.
    Are facts not flowers
        and flowers facts
or poems flowers
        or all works of the imagination,
            interchangeable?

At that point I was cut off.
My lady had to leave me and see where the boys had disappeared to. When she got back the water was boiling and I'd put the book down. I thought instead of the things around me. How fleeting they all are and how they will all eventually perish: from the tinder dry grass to the oleander whose scent escapes me as soon as I get any distance from it, and the boys, who in time won't need me to hold them back from the bluff's edge; even the dialects that corrupt my search for the just word—
    the love
              beneath this longing for permanence
makes me sit in awe at the foot of a rock wall that will last long past any lines of imagination etched into pages fated to rot before my efforts to find those lines' roots
       stretch back
             and, with hope, forward
like the horizon seen from a windy cliff,
       lasting at least
             as long
as this mythic light reflected off the water
       here at earth's center.

Mediterraneo 2

Dawn's rosy fingers: like a certain look
               of star-baked rage
                                and wrath
ready to slash the sea's oil sleek skin.

This cruise ship rumbles
               under ink incising
pages full of poems may as well lay waste
to moments better spent
               not reading into them,
not even observing
               for the sake of some aesthetic exchange,
but living
               in another life's reflection:

the Son   of One   I am.

Attis was imported from the east
(as were most "religious abominations")—
a pine fed by his own
                       emasculation's blood rite,
re-enacted each spring by castratti priests,
               and felled yearly
                       till our Lord
of the Cross (another tree)
             hung in the balance—ours
—to rectify accounts
accrued by civilization's
                       having gotten out of hand.

This with the open tomb—
                       root of all relinking...

There is no corner of the world unknown to us.
The bar's television informs everywhere's all.
I can lie at the ship's pool, next to the beauty center,
ice cream in hand, sniff suntan lotion, and listen

to ladies talk of battles with cellulite as I ponder
Paul's voyages, hanging by his vision
on the road to Damascus now
would be considered a hallucination.

What would Attis
              have me be
                            if not a vine,
a Dionysian rhizome encroaching
           on the house-
holder's duties
                      to intoxicate and confuse.

He would take me to Cybele's sanctuary,
              have me grasp the nearest sword
and, in a frenzy of cymbals and drums,
          cut my cock and balls off;
whence I would wrap myself around the pine
              like a violet wreath
                        to worship
root and branch
        amid our over-brimming
                        parasitic pleasures,
our abundance.

August holidays by the sea.
The windsurfer pulls the sail tight to catch a levantine breath and feel the self-satisfaction speed generates. The tennis player strokes with topspin to sharpen the ball's dip and send it more quickly out of reach. The drinker sips aperitifs with a consort on the terrace of a café beside the old port, admiring catamarans, prows, schooners, sloops and yawls. The dreamer feeds torpid evenings with zodiac excursions, periplum of the tongue's edge, *periplum, not as land looks on a map but as sea bord seen by men sailing.* Or on the beach, the lover thieving glances at breasts aspiring to the earth one infers in them (gravity

being a feminine force), breasts not thieved with
any lewd intent but culled to bestow upon a single
lady all the lactescent vessels in sight and daydream
Ephesian Diana into the scandal magazines strewn
on beach towels. Or the watcher simply gazing at
satellites as they cruise through the churning Milky
Way to echoes of a discotheque across the bay...

Even ecstasy
        has been synthesized
                        in tablet form!

Were but the imagination and not
        the nervous system a valid source
                for religious rapture
I would gladly accept Nana's or any other's
                virgin labor.
And even this
        plastic world I could make
                with the mind's electric
a fit place for my son's reflections

in the water.   We spread
                a fluid grace
of information
far beyond the root,
        so far
that even where sunsets are such snapshot
occasions
we can only hope   to remember
        the death of a god
               ever surging in anemones,
in fields of poppy sleep,
        or roses,
        photos even,   and poems
gathering dust with a heap of myths.

Quadri Toscani: Monte Cetona

1.

Plush sunflower field
foreshortened yellow
against flat sunrise.
Hips silhouetted
against cotton dress.

2.

Cicadas shriek.
Boy chucks pebbles
into bucket of water,
runs back to gravel
path and picks more
up off his shadow.
Sun slants left to right.

3.

Fig issues its pearl
drop as if desiring
to be picked—skin
opened and eaten
across a clean chin.

4.

Veiled sunburst
stripes through clouds.
Cross atop the mountain.
Queen bee comes in
from under the eaves.

5.

Cypress trees bite
into dusk, drunk
on still clustered wine
flowing below. Rows
of olives and vineyards.

6.

Half moon rises. Moths
or maybe humming birds
(hard to see in evening
light) feed on four-o'clocks.
Rusty farm implements.
Castle lit on the hill.

7.

Dogs bark. We
keep warm and watch
for shooting stars.
Tree stump serves
as altar, absorbs
our dew in its rings
after we leave.

Portofino
for Dino Betti Van Der Noot

1.

This sea—silent
or so it seems
after ocean

surf undercut land's edge
lights in distance
glimmering against Pound's collage:

sea
central to the journey's
centripetal drift

homeward through
olives terraced up and over
moonlit hills

    2.

bird song
links boat to lemon tree
overcast

with somber gaps
the silences of an urbane life
by the fireside

two women talking
of houses and cancer
quietly

3.

a man seated
smoking a pipe with his coffee
holds

a handful of colored pencils
in his fist
as he draws

the hills
above this fine port
waves

hardly lapping
the lungomare's understated
spread

of restaurants
and price tags off-season
slashed on sportswear

he
thinks, perhaps, how wave weight
corresponds to water mass

proportionally and
how the ocean
could wash all this finery away

his happiness now
confined to gaps
a workweek allows

to reflect on
ways untaken, compromises
made and risks missed

he (in front of me)
projects bits of his vision
with swift strokes

contained in a
book can be carried
wherever

and looked at
time permitting should
the soft life's reflection

inspire apnea
or

       4.

slate quarried
from black hills
behind this one

and white
marble from Carrara heavy
with memory

(if you can call it
that) Michelangelo's rough-hewn
blocks floating downriver

toward Rome or Florence
all part
of a home forever under construction

as the memory
of what it was like before
this house was

here the oranges and mimosa's
yellow balls in bloom and
cemetery somewhere near

5.

reading by light
reflected off

the sea you face
each year

another Odyssey
back to Ithaca

reading of battles in a
morning spied on by

the buddhas
over the fireplace

echoes
of last night

telling us all how
you shiatsued yourself

off prozac even though
erano sciazzi tuoi

some voice must be
entering the gaps

between lines reminding us
amid the olives

and ivy and odor
of eucalyptus seeds

burning in a hearth
the value of laughter

and touch

6.

house surrounds

once wild roses
bezeled
in a wall of jasmine

boar dugouts along terrace edge
native pines
their smoke's odor and the oak

still
hangs brown leaves
that withered last

fall but wouldn't
waiting till spring's
cherries blossom

a virgin
variation
on the green theme

as if
to show us
who are capable of wondering

we are
not the only ones
attempt to defy time

Love in a Tuscan Light: Easter Sunday

Gregorian

In that place, where memory stays
and takes its state, triggered by pictures
admired once for the new way
they treated the changing light,

now hanging from museum walls
or shut in heavy books on coffee tables
to entertain and distract guests
with any number of nostalgias;

where medieval towns atop hills,
immured behind ochre stones, lord
over the frayed links with a history
feeding our indifference to Amor;

in that place we feast to forget. And after
wine and truffles and wild boar,
the bread-and-water-fed plague centuries
surge to the fore in senescent streaks

that break through stray clouds;
and your lover's lips seem even more
inviting when they reflect an idol
long written off as outmoded,

a myth worthy of suffering old mothers
whose wayward sons have gone off
to make their fortunes in a ladyless world
off the pages of airport romances.

But as the clouds change form
in the course of a day you know: the new
green that blinds you now will turn
gold in summer, brown in winter. Such

is the repetition of sacred themes
scaped in the land. Such the procession
of paschal shadows across the valley, as if
a master's hand had stroked the sun's rays

into existence. Today we remember
how one man reclaimed love's face;
while here, in fields within earshot
of the sweet new style's meter,

clouds clear, off and on, as they have
for centuries, to bare the work of men
and women in a new light—always just
a theme repeated faithfully over time.

Julian

setback two mountains between
aquavelvet coat cloudburst ambition
cliff-hung silhouette panorama
dug tensile in olive leaf sheen

silver laurel sticks implicate
pseudo-brickface train graffiti
dense under espalier and
wisteria charged puddle skin

hark back spud nose buffer
canticle lick abscessed slide show
rock fort interring slush fun
mulberry picking memory project

inured blithely absent-winded
health-cared but disc slipped
synapse jump in sweat pinch
tension wire less beatrix screen

night blood bandit aftermath pass
go lamb chop true thorn skewered
sunflower field seed feast furrow
mud outjump boy foot rubber soul

overpass road rage network blind
side jostling wood clacks to exorcise
amnesiate old-style-wise commemoration
of death beats death Son rise

Blue

The Boat

Sea air breeds a light
within
            waking
from a long season of city gray.

Even the shadows here are blue.

I show a boy his first sight
of a boat's bow cleaving through a sea
            (a topos central
      to both blood and affection)
seething a streak of celestial foam
            in its wake.

The Beach

Two in the afternoon:
Seagull brushes us with his shadow.
Eat urchins on the rock—only the females'
      orange aphrodisiac eggs
      arranged in a star.

Misha sets out to collect every strip of alga
      washed up in the bay.
He arranges them in the letters
      of his own language and needs
      to know the names of things.

Ruben digs a cavern out of the sand
      and sets up an army of divers.
Maybe in a thousand hundred years, he says,
I'll be big enough to enter.

You part your legs a little
to let the sun hit the insides of your thighs.
After a while you walk into the water,
nipples stiffening in the wind, and wade
to your navel as I sit reading *terza rima*:
Pasolini's landscapes of odors and flesh
exulted to the level of religious longing.
You wait and wade in the wind,
hesitate unwittingly for the poet's breath,
plunge in and are transfigured—
from a shivering girl with arms crossed
over her breasts out of embarrassment,
to a sleek line of skin cutting
just under the surface of the sea.
Your strokes—impeccable. Barely a splash
as you freestyle so far out you are
a spot of flesh against the vast blue.
Backstroke: windmill moving parallel
with the shore, poised fingers pointing
sunward, circling back behind you
to allow the other hand to fly.
Breaststroke: arms opening outward,
head bobbing in and out of the water
for breath. When you rise to your feet I follow
the line from between the cleft of your breasts
down to your navel. Your flanks flare out
gently against the sharp light.
I know no rime could do justice to the stride
you use to approach me. No words, yet I try.
For though this scene may be repeated,
it feels willed by a breath drenched
in a blue I've never seen before.

Island

The gulls send out alarms when we intrude
on their island. They think we've come
to take their babies away (a delicacy here).

Jelly fish pink in ankle-deep water.
The Shark's Rock bites into the horizon.
Wild garlic and *erisimo* in the breeze.

Our skin burns in the sun as we eat
on the deck of a prow with a lateen sail.
I lay my head on your thigh and listen

to your pulse under the wind lapping
water's edge against piles of dry algae.
I imagine your lips behind the bikini's bulge.

Later, out in the gulf, the captain
marries us and we dive off the boat. I rush
back before I lose confidence in the water.

You follow me later with your smooth strokes.

Picasso

I keep thinking of Picasso.
His blue paintings. Not the sad,
early ones of the so-called "blue period,"
full of worldly melancholy
and gaunt resignation in the faces and poses;
but the ones he painted
just after the Second World War
in Antibes, on the Mediterranean shore,
where he had sought refuge.
The bather series

I've heard them called, full
of sky blue and flesh
and playful misshapen human figures
frolicking in the sand.

These were the happiest
days of his life, I say to myself
whenever I see them. You can tell
he had just fallen in love.
The Mediterranean must have reminded him
of that love for life
that had nursed him in his youth.

And here is a simile
I've never thought of before:
She, the Mediterranean, is like
a generous wet nurse,
feeding babies raised in their parents'
cult of tragedy
with her own blue love
of wonder, the warm
salt-spray taste of summer
on her bosom.

We saw one of those paintings
together in Antibes.
"The Joy of Life" it was called.
The same day you walked with me on the beach,
barefoot, your high heels dangling from your
hands, and we stole touches of hidden skin
and drank up the sun.

Valley of the Moon

I take you across
the sharp rocks—again
your heels in your hands,
feeling the way
with your feet
through the moonlit craters.
I lay my jacket over a flat rock,
sit you down
and open your black dress.
Your lips glisten
in the moonlight one day shy of full
and draw my tongue to them
as if they were part of my own
body as well.

How you see the stars,
the big dipper, and the Saracen tower
under it, overlooking
the sea's midnight sheen
when I enter you—again
and again.

Crags

Walk barefoot down the path
and feel
        the stones under my soles—
each one triggering a rush
the shod life denies.

Sit on a rock
        to marvel
and read the depths

into degrees of azure
and aquamarine.

A starfish's blinding orange
        (opposite color) between two rocks,
languishing
as if to embody contrast.

Horizon

Ship moves
                through dawn's rose.
Approaches,
                touches the sun.

Doesn't burn.

Rocks 1

Robust front line
cliff-cuts upper strata,
strikes solemn, hard-edged,
with swift incision.

Risk asked of first
comes distinct as sound
redoubles a feel forced
on siren-pierced heels.

Echo accelerates, winds
rabble mass and horde
round wistful shades
to stilt their own hours.

Rocks 2

Stark diagonal edges strike—
marble streaked and stuck
between dark cross-strokes—
pressure and dead age.

Plumb against grain
of sacrifice and treasure
assuring a wedge
headlong into heaven

as on earth exactly.
Salt spume tingles
in a throat whose voice
this vital shuttle emits.

Rocks 3

Breaks bellow sheer
up scaled precipices,
sever softened footholds
rent by white ascesis.

Dense conglomerate forms
founder, fade into piecemeal
fantod scaffolds wrought
of restless insight.

Racked and roiled,
distant cracks crowd
grounded wraiths in ranks
to seal a rear front.

Rocks 4

Wind whips into wave-
and-weather etched rifts.
Wonder's tongue divulges
its absent offering.

Stiff consonant grafts
scratch surfaces intimately,
like scars, bar entrance
into the cavern mouth—

withholding a mineral trance.
Hushed barriers swallow
serried sentry cusps
whole in humble updrafts.

Ruins at Seliunte

Eating pistachios on the altar
of a Greek temple by the sea.

A black and white dog
comes begging for morsels,

crunches even the shells
(though he looks well fed).

Find shelter from the wind
behind a wall, light a cigarette.

A herd of sheep grazes amid
heaps of scattered columns.

Wild parsley grows between
the crumbling stones—some

still hinting at their golden section.

Anonymous Painting

Woman wipes Christ's face
as he carries his cross
in a light that barely
shows the blood muddied
by centuries of smoke.

Soft sepia intimation
of a horror inherent
in this innate impulse:
to catch the true image
of God's betrayal—

make it mystery in a transept
so quiet you can hear
the whispers of admirers and
echoes of a faith's heels.

Each evening's history
boasts an eternal return:
the chestnut leaf falling at my feet,
the round cobblestones between bars and art galleries
     by the church droning
          old ladies' Ave Marias,
the stretch of breast
        under the arm
in a nude photo drawing me up and out
    till the touch
that fulfills the process in what follows
     when I see you again.

conditions

———//———

If I found blood in this rock
would you make me a museum?

If the sun carved my face
would I be worthy of the spectacle?

If the theater unleashed
in this layered mind
fled like a nomad into the steppe,
would you grant me respite

from death, the all-embracing death
our petty dreams allude to?

If the fear I harbor in my cells
exploded into words—logos—
would you let it be read

when I'm gone,
when not even the ruins
can attest to my exile?

metal heavy   burning air

The Telling

to just
take
the time
it takes
to tell
how
time has
held
me in
its grip
and be
rid
of it

Opium

A dream to languish
in a language
that is dream:
a history of wishes, itches,
tingles and approaches
to a peace that passes
into vivid sleep.

Watching the Welder

sparks
that blind
too bright to resist

and if
there were more things
to bind

The Old Bricklayer

Balanced up there
at the ladder's top step,
his fat-handed palette knife
caresses the trowel.
His body is still
strong but stiff
from years of walls
he's come to resemble.

The Jewel

Each cut
brings the stone
closer
to its pure form,
closer
to the restive light
longing
to flee.

Each facet
frees
rays that breed
others,
braiding to generate
the splendor
you know is natural
only
by its flaws.

Three Ways of Describing a Persimmon

1) It's like
a tomato that doesn't know it's not
supposed to be sweet.

2) Something you wrote when you wrote like
you sometimes
wish you could write.

3) The seed of a dream
dreamt in a familiar country
you still haven't been to, or heard of.

——//——

You are beautiful
but
I like you ugly
so
I can see
what I believe
comes from within
through
your withering
skin.

Verse in Search of an Anthology

Instead of writing
this poem I
could be sleeping
or talking to friends or
praying or meditating
or fucking or
hurting someone I love
or thinking of
others' suffering;
but here I am
gauging line breaks
for some soul
on the margins
yearning to break loose
from the carcass
that makes poets write.

Baudelaire

When the bad flowers come out
I know it's time to chuck

some spleen into the rain
and hang with the itch

reading sacred writ
into the flaking facades

of a riverless city, somewhere
between throat and groin.

When the bad flowers come out
you gotta kick against the prick

bearing down on you with his light.

After Creeley

Tonight, the holding
back
to a burning bush.

A flute climbs
scales
of traffic in the rain.

This allusion:
to a dark
sidereal fire
reason
is unable to restrain.

After Derrida

give in terms
against for
giving is not
possible in
the economy
of a market
where ideas for-
give their own
inadequacies
as possible
for against
a discourse on
quotidian things
there is an
escape that is
the heart as
can't be set
in dialectic

Nowhere Near Pont Mirabeau

Her hair she combs
           like the hair of the dead
facades blocking the Seine Celan's
too-dense verse
              disappeared in
There
this life's become the same place
and traces of an assassin language wash
      up on the quai:
                  "Wer,
wenn ich schriee..."

Hear me: books mean nothing
where ellipses betray
the whisper of uninvited angels

Fourier's grave
harmony interred on Mount Martyr
under buds of yellow weed trees
these cities
        have numbed me to
This Paris, especially,
a sprawl of cerebral convolutions
reading texts thrown to the river,
zapping channels on rue St. Denis to reveal
a fat woman's winged lips
touched by Pan's cock or
shit-eating rituals in lingerie
no library or museum could snuff
          a candle to...

Where
the source sprung before one God's name
                was uttered
    carried back
against the curbstone's gutteral flow
to glimpse that bridge impulse

nowhere near any child's first phonemes
        spittling off chaotic tongue
to comb the dross at river's bed
                                redeeming
Where
a city indulges in its own elegy
who would hear
                    how beautifully light,
like the face of a boy you might once have been
nowhere near any bridge
            that stiffens this will to live

After Tolstoy

Looking for that
true sentence. It
begins: *As always...*
and ends only
when the thing
rings true on its own,
itself an action,
and cloaks everything
around it—like
...there was no way
he could ever see
her as she once was.

Waterfall

1.

Beer-colored cascade foams
without writing
rainbow over pool

2.

Current funnels
between two rocks
eddy full of leaches

3.

Leaf shadows mist
through ambitions
empty drift up

4.

Bugs hover behind lens
gnats, dragonflies, mosquitoes
wind nearly flips page

5.

Initials etched in rocks
tree roots rending
rust-streaked granite mass

6.

Iron laden water
cools jaundiced feet
need for seething sleep

7.

Pines loom over
cliffs bitter with youth's
missed opportunities

8.

Dam beyond falls
skimmed off lake top
depth as absent as time

9.

Shale layers reflect
sun's intimate approximation
of it in its rays

10.

Relentless din smoothing
edges rifted out long
before this paper was seed

The Lure of the Exotic

Something about the women
in Tahiti
led Gaugin to extended exile.

Maybe their "unaffected grace
and communal ease,"
as the caption under the painting says.

Or maybe their caramel skin—
the heat of it at dawn
or the cool midday caresses
under the sun.
                Or maybe
just the seed
of something sweet as mango—

so sweet
against the backdrop of a drab Cartesian grid
it draws a man further
and further from the strains
of gray and aging

toward a distant sex
colored within him all along.

Ten-year-ago Photo

Your face looks
like you knew
it'd be the only one
I'd have to look at.

Insight

Every night
I go to sleep
with the hope
that you will come
to my door
in the morning
and let me show you
how the river
changes day by day
from the green-gray
of the rains
to the turquoise
of your eyes
at dawn.

Gloria in Paris

I'm writing this on the back
of a tattered copy of my passport.
This is just to say my lines
have dropped out. My borders
blurred to the point of exhaustion,
a whole century of light
having passed through unnoticed.
So many reassuring structures:
the family, the state, the university,
the church; they've all been condemned
over cigarettes, coffee and wine.
And that's fine—even funny.
Because this judgement must wait
for us to live out our lives—
what they cling to and cleave:
your inherited lines, and my
waning structures of mind.

Conversation with a Writer
for B.C.

She told me about her book,
The Face of the Goddess,
about the making of a film
about a jungle deity.
The main character is a young woman,
the film's producer.
While she was shooting
she got raped in the jungle
in front of the goddess' altar.
The writer tells me about a scene
in which the young woman
can feel the blade of a machete
between her shoulder blades.
She tells me about the rape
and how the young woman—
afraid for her life,
with a knife to her throat,
surrounded by five banditos
—is told not to tell anyone.
And in a stroke of inspiration,
the young woman says:
"I won't tell anyone. But you also
have to promise not to tell anyone."
And she lets them fuck her.
And they become sweet with her,
even give her back some money.
And the writer tells me all this
in the third person,
after a civil dinner, and
I listen, suggesting options
for structural approaches, and give
encouragement, always referring
to the main character as "she" or "her"
or "the girl"—never "you." Even though
it's clear it's the writer's own story.
And that's what she wants
me to know.

Waiting for the Yellow Buses
for Dareuscha

There were always
a few minutes to kill
standing by the road—
Lackawack Rd. we called it
when we first got there.
Then in time they gave it
a number: Route 55 West.
In any case, we were always—
and still are—way early.
First bus 2 would pass by
with its yellow top as flat
as Mr. Havrish's crewcut
(that stutter still gives me
the creeps when I remember it).
Then came bus 8, ours,
the short stubby bee bus
that looked cut in half.
What were we doing there?
The nearby prison
loomed over the landscape
just to remind us
we were free.
And how mama and tato
came to be free.
But of course there's always
a prison somewhere nearby
just to remind you
your freedom could be worse.
When I don't feel
grateful, I feel doomed
by the freedom we were told
made anything possible
for us. Yet with all
the sacrificial love we got,
we would've no doubt done well
even on the other side
of the iron curtain. You

would've probably wound up
some high-level apparatchik;
and I'd either be drinking
with the poets
in the writers union,
or dry with paperless writers
in the psycho ward, inspired
by something real
to rebel against.
But that's pure speculation.
What we have today
are the buses that came
to us from exotic places
with names like Sundown,
Peekamoose and Shandaken,
or Lackawack and Neversink.
And how the hell
did we wind up in Napanoch,
"place of many waters"?
We fished sunnies and catfish
together by the dam
behind the paper mill,
the one that poisoned us
with PCBs, and mama
cooked them up for us.
That dam was where I got
my first initiation into drugs.
The buses would come
from places where the "hickies"
were so isolated that they'd had
to inbreed. (It was long after
Napanoch that I realized why
Clifford Faust had no chin.)
I'd wait with you in mid-winter,
my parted-in-the-middle hair
still wet, not worrying
about catching cold.

Then we'd climb on,
and you'd repeat the jokes
told by Lucy Ricardo or Archie
Bunker—tato's own chair
vacant till the weekend,
no male to blame
for setting me straight.
I'd get so alone
over the years. And it hit
home much later how
you are the only one
who knows what waiting
for the buses meant:
killing time with you before
having to deal with a world
where the high-pitched love
we got wasn't visible. Sister,
my life is nearly half over,
and I feel now I'm opening
a vault full of jewels
only you can see—
jewels made of dreams,
laughter and tears
The rattle of wooden planks
on the old bridge whenever
we'd go *cherez pole*
(through the fields) to church.
You always knew what season
it was by the corn's height.
And then there was the mystery
of the lobster carcasses—
the gastronomic self-effacement
we fed on that helped
make us impermeable
and tough-willed to a fault.
Or the dogs, how many dogs?
German shepherds tainted

with Eastern European paranoia.
Princess' eye after the fight
with Aza (what dog
could live up to Aza, the first?).
Or Shakey's swollen head
bobbing every which way
like a dashboard decoration
(did we like her because we knew
she was doomed?).
And let's not forget
the Barringers' poodles—
the white-trash mascots
that sped us out of Napanoch…
Still, Route 55 brought a certain
comfort (and still does),
especially after a summer of camp,
where the sound of marching
inspired an early taste of despair.
You were my only anchor there.
By inviting me in to kill
a few minutes in the afternoons
between marches, letting me
relax in the girls' barracks,
full of powders and perfumes,
and catch my breath
after having to be tough
for the first time, you held
my hands when my world
was spilling through them—
and thus set me up for life.

Tato

That last photo of you—
the one where your dewlapped neck
stands out because you lost weight
(because you cut down on the drink
because you were killing yourself)—
shows you as old as ever, waiting
nobly for death with a resigned glint
in those blue eyes veiled by sagging
Asiatic lids and bifocal lenses.
Those blue eyes helped save you
from the war… Though now it shows:
your skin—framed by linen white hair—
is still olive, and your nose and mouth
now bring out the wandering half-Jew
you never managed to deny
in so much devotion to a Holy Mother.

Figure at the Top of the Stairs

Whoever it is
up those stairs

I yearn for you
to ease me into a sleep

I'll recognize
in morning light

as a sleep
worthy of another life

when at once
my eyes open

and I know
you are no longer there

but among all
those I'll meet

in my day.

Moving Again

The commuter train rumbles
                with me wound tight in its fist,
past the city's drab industrial
                edge, to the mountains for a tryst

with my self. It's been too long
                since I've spent any time
with the source of all wrong
                in me. I've been blinded

steadily by the static routine
                of office hours and family meals
I considered so unseemly
                when my life was on wheels.

Now I strain to move on any whim,
though I must—or let the light go dim.

I have seen glimpses of an eye
at night; it works its way
into my field of vision and brings
with it dreams of drowning
at a site once meant
                              for sacrifices.

This eye is all of me my mind
has been able to accept, above
and below the line of consciousness
we know does not really exist;
                              it is gray,

the eye, and at times it turns
silver when I am light or can
reflect in ways I normally can not
                              imagine…

how it reads the language
whose alphabet I am always
                              forgetting

as soon as daybreak orders insight
                              into writ.

Metastasis

We have only just
initiated the process: First
the skin reacts to the sun,
then withers. And it is
good. The air turns acrid.
We breathe apocalyptic
dreams into a daily routine
that removes them so we
can function. And that too
is good. Because all
this information overwhelms
in a way that bleeds
innocence with a barely benign
cartoon-like indifference.
Almost like the bloody
sculpture of Christ so big
on the cross that my boy
is afraid to go near it.
He asks me, "What
is he doing?" And I say,
"He's dying," and try to slip
past the next inevitable
question: "Why?"—knowing
I'll just say, "Because
that's the way it is."
Or maybe, "To redeem us."
And how could I ever
explain—even to myself—that
I feel that's right?
And all the words
and screams that come after
are just glosses
on that first skin
line waiting now
for the cells to run amok.

Airports and the Thing That Smells Like Fear

There's some unholy business going down.
Fast food chain gangs and furtive glances.
My man's got broken glass in his eyes
and a soldering iron for a tongue.

The Terror is where the virgins are—
gazelle-eyed houris wiping plastic counter tops
with the last paper towel stolen
from the rack that severed the thief's hand.

A ticket stings the lint that feeds a pocket;
and the breed of men who die for God
are far from dying out behind their sunglasses.

The dawn, and other such initiations, wills
a new look at this age's errant light
and all the irritant shadows it incurs.

An Afternoon with Andy Warhol
and Abu Musab al-Zarqawi

Saturday afternoon where the "in" crowd hangs out.
I stumble on a Warhol exhibit: an armchair,
a couch, and six TVs playing his films
full of pretty boys, softcore porn, transsexuals
and other assorted trash.

I sit down to read my *Financial Times*
about the head of "Monotheism and Holy War":
the man who's been beheading everyone on video
and raising hell all over the world.

With my pink paper and uncut hair,
I've become an installation.

I, too, am glamorous and cool.

In my own private factory, I, too,
raise hell in the world.

If I Told You Death Was Just

If I told you death
      was just you
not being where
      what died is
I would be as dead
      as last year's
leaves come to me
      in the air
I breathe now feeling
      so alive.

Because the sun
is full of blood
the moon rose
a glowering ball

leaving the sea
awash in its light
wake bleeding off
oil smooth sheen.

Begin we again
the skin's intimate
insistence, sand
and salt, the wonder

that binds us
to a life of fire,
sacrifice disguised
as wind. We move

giving in and out
a heat of words
wet with shadows
bliss will dispel.

On Leaving

Did I tell you
I wanted to be
alone.

Did I tell you
there was no room
for both me
and my mind
in this home.

Did I show you
the sacrifice
I keep like a trophy
on the mantle.

Did I give you
cause
to resent me.

Have I hurt you.
Are you there.
Can you hear
how I'm struggling
against the bond
I hold dear.

Will you be
here when I go
and return.

And if I return,
will you will
as you did
when I told you
I would?

dependent
redemptions

———//———

Who woke up this morning
    before dawn to the cry of children?

Who woke up this morning before dawn
    with dreams of scorched earth?

Who woke up this morning, before dawn,
    wanting yesterday's twilight—
    when the want had momentarily subsided?

Before dawn full of angels' absence.

Dawn on Sunday full of clouds,
    soon the church bells...

Who woke up this morning before dawn
    was not who went to sleep.

Death and resurrection are enfolded in every dream.
The self in conflict with the self
    writes private screams to disarm.

In dream

we pass
from screen to screen,

through scenes
we know
we've acted out
before—
        we've been...

It seems
this can't be real;

still we feel
the play of light
directs our minds
to react.

We become attached
as a moth attracts
              its flame;

though we realize
just the same,
we are nothing

but the light

looking for the dreamer
through a thick night.

Change Up

I once wrote poems
exalting things
most don't feel exist:

like Mohamed weeping
in a mist
of insect wings

or fish in sinks
scaling slippers
stolen from a whore.

But now I write
about the world—
or love sometimes

when aroused
to doubt what's real
to write about…

and pray
        more and more.

No

no home for me this world no more
the ground beneath my feet my cradle
grave will be once burnt

endless motion instressed fords what
no rooted fool dare sow or set
to cult when winds converge things still

disrupt all patterns insought
to out a fugitive strife with wont
for place is same and soul alone

upset by distances the lines between
here and there the blurry rite
I deign name through jaded ways

where ink-stained blank admits to nil

Dependent Redemptions

to intimate between leaves
a green-obsessed
                charge
spring on the skin absolves

or whisper tendrilled letters
this flesh's lost alphabet
        alludes to
through a shriven passage

and slake some wistful rush
assailed
        by swallows circling
to devour an insect legacy

at dusk a castle such
as vanishes with intent
            to feed
particulars contingent on an image

ordered, formed, redeemed
                and graced
to guide a common touch
through burgeoning and waste

―――//―――

Learning language as if
learning to approximate
the lean of an ear toward
the roar of a crowd
in a game with no commentary:
just the crescendo and de-
crescendo of a drone
whose meaning only masses
are privy to, waiting
to take orders, to be told
what to do when
the vibrating link between
membrane, bone and breath we
instinctively obey breaks…

———//———

The language that sustains
        a word kept, a lie reveled in
        as imagination, a tensile myth—
the process whereby apples rot
        in the fruit basket,
thistles overgrow in the closets,
fricatives turn to voiced alveolars,
thick gives way to dick
        fat sound-forests
        tendering emotional charges—
a story meaningfully unrolled
        as foolscap folded
        into swan or turned key…
opening out to initiate
        dry dreams
walking sleep-ridden through light.

After Ibn Arabi

Even the heedless
scream of a child bears
a light so intense
it overpowers the senses
and is seen only
when focused shrill on the ear.

Patience, and you'll hear
the name of your Lord
howling the power
you pursue, yet fear.

After Psalm 104

He touches the hills
and they smoke,

looks at the earth
and it trembles

under the feet
of a man unable to see

how, in our fractured
state, we can hope

to speak of One
so beyond He is

beyond even belief.

> *"Which of the Lord's bounties*
> *do you and you deny?"* —The Koran, Sura 55

The tower, in the tarot,
is divine intervention,
                terror on the street.

Bricks fall, girders melt,
victims leave their tasks in a panicked leap—
      and nothing
         is said of their faith.

The dust of burnt bodies
        gets on your shoes.

The city lumbers to get back to normal.
Reluctant grins peer out from the pall.

An area of destruction
        a waking slap in the face
                      and forces
at work that flout the simple-minded rhetoric.

This bounty is given to insight:
wine and song last through the night,
compensate for drudgery
        on crosswalks gridlocked by the blind.

Wash my eyes—oh messenger!—of exile's dust.
Whisper to me things
      no man or jinn has uttered
and I will be banished from my self,
                            annihilated,
        nothing without the Lord
—may His name leash me aloft like smoke!

For without my own *fana*-tic
      leap in the darkness
I char under the gaze of my zealous guides.

———//———

Lord—again this trite
epithet. I need to work
an image of your rite
and make a world

to order that disturbed
store of fragments—
without it seeming ordered,
forced, stiff and spent.

But the rigid poem
is also an icon;
and though not open,
its sense rests on

form as symbol meant
to be seen through.
Order heals the rent
screen I make of you,

that I can call you
You—open to any me.

Jesus

You're all I know,
all I have to give.
The rest is just a game
played in a labyrinth.
I make my art
for no one to buy
and claim my art
to be my life?
I work to live,
and live to love,
and pray for all
to be integral?
Though I like the play,
I prefer the passion
and would rather lose
than win and revel
in such success as
makes me lose you.
I prefer to be nothing
in this race
as long as I can give
a glimpse
of your dead face
to those alive—
that they may be
as dead as you.
And for that I'd
play at being
stiff-alive as they.

things here

1.

Things here
always happen
edgewise,
slanted off browshade
in shafts
careening down mindeaves
to shatter
across deltas
the heart's muscles
have squeezed and sucked
into submission,
away from shards of light
absorbed
by hidden sleep
and hardened
by a life
wrung of all sense

2.

Things here
seem like
what links empty space
to longing
for lost melodies,
falling rain
to the metallic clang
of hunger

always wanting

the craven eye
to cease its rampant circles

and feast
rather
with the lambent blood's
flow
over redemptive fire

3.

Things here break
down
as soon
as the turn
outruns the pride
that wells up
in dropping it

each sin
contests
that it isn't that:
neither a dead
category
nor the guilt
vestigial of a tired
callus
some civilization formed
through friction

4.

Things here
take time
from storage
spaces
full of accumulated
merit

they bleed
metaphysical propositions
that drive you
to penetrate
membranes
ignorant of good
and evil, Latin
or Greek

5.

Things here
aren't so clear

if it weren't for this life
lust
I'd be elsewhere
now
digging through dead
books maybe
or talking
about talking and its degrees
of separation

from the idea
of you
to the in-you that
binds

6.

Things here
rip through me
and stun
like the cold thump
of a skull
hitting hard cement
in my chest

somewhere
there's been a mistake

take me away
from all this physical love

I might
finally
be ready to leave

7.

Things here
don't stand
scrutiny
with one eye closed

the depth
that draws
our gaze waits
for us
to gall ourselves
raw

and against
all odds

the gold looks
flat
when you have
everything
and the touch
is still of the dream
you've just awoken
from

8.

Things here
allow me
to see the sky
and not worry
that the green
out my window
breathes
at me
a sheen my future
won't remember
and fall

leaves of my past
will tread
hard
on the burn
in a rusted
trash can

9.

Things here
mean so little in
relation
to what's between
the foot and
its trace in the climb

both
read the distance
between
them as essential
to their
straying

in a place
where tricks
play the mind
each way
of the step

10.

Things here
make it clear
that life's too
short

so many languages
still slip
past my ears
so many lovers
and wives still
only
imagined

cutting bread
or looking at me
in the mirrors
of a never-seen-before
yet familiar
home

Made in the USA
Middletown, DE
26 November 2024